Sylvia

Always ~~Rely~~

Jessica x

WE me! WITHOUT YOU

LISA SWERLING
& RALPH LAZAR

CHRONICLE BOOKS
SAN FRANCISCO

LIBRARY OF CONGRESS CATALOGING-IN-PUBLICATION
DATA AVAILABLE.

ISBN 978-1-4521-2232-8

MANUFACTURED IN CHINA

10 9 8 7 6 5 4 3 2 1

CHRONICLE BOOKS LLC
680 SECOND STREET
SAN FRANCISCO, CA 94107
WWW.CHRONICLEBOOKS.COM

LIKE CRAFTS
WITHOUT
GLUE

YODEL—AY
WITHOUT
HEE—HOO

BOLT
WITHOUT
SCREW

OLD MACDONALD
WITHOUT
MOO

LIKE APPLE
WITHOUT
BITE

BOO
WITHOUT
FRIGHT

CLOUD
WITHOUT
WHITE

DAY
WITHOUT
SUNLIGHT

me
WE WITHOUT YOU?
THERE'S NO
WAY!

LIKE WAITER
WITHOUT
TRAY

ELEPHANT
WITHOUT
GRAY

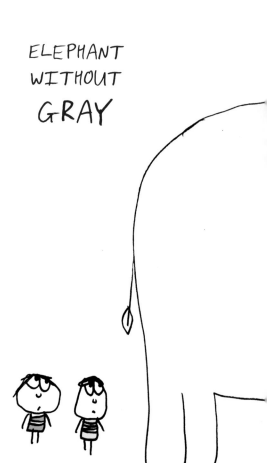

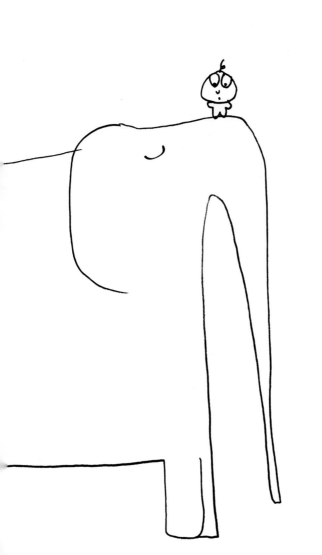

HORSE
WITHOUT
HAY

FRENCH
WITHOUT
BERET

DISCO
WITHOUT
DJ

DOH
WITHOUT
PLAY

HIP,
HIP . . .

WITHOUT
HOORAY

me
WE WITHOUT YOU?
WHAT A
BORE!

LIKE KITE
WITHOUT
SOAR

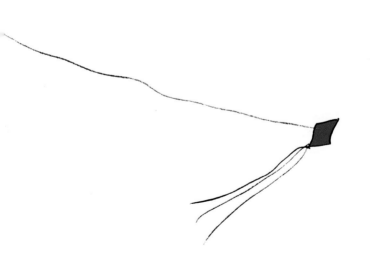

HOUSE
WITHOUT
DOOR

ROWBOAT
WITHOUT
OAR

SOCCER
WITHOUT
SCORE

GOLF
WITHOUT
FORE!

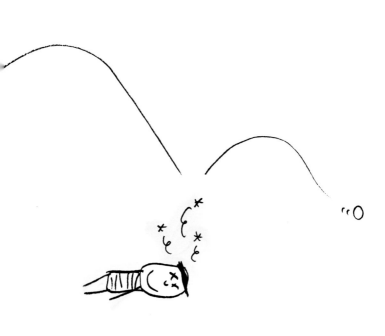

LION
WITHOUT
ROAR

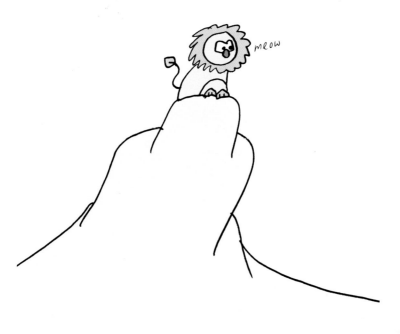

ICE CREAM
WITHOUT

MORE!

PLAYGROUND
WITHOUT
EXPLORE

we
WE WITHOUT YOU?
HOW COULD THAT
BE?

LIKE ALPHABET
WITHOUT
A, B, C

BIRTHDAY
WITHOUT
HAPPY

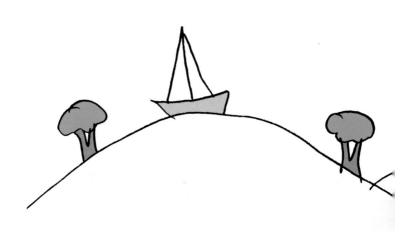

EARTH
WITHOUT
SEA

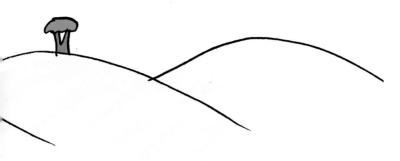

DO, RE
WITHOUT
MI

WE WITHOUT YOU?
IT DOESN'T MAKE
SENSE!

LIKE HIPPIE
WITHOUT
INCENSE

FARM
WITHOUT
FENCE

WE WITHOUT YOU?
AN IMPOSSIBLE
THING!

LIKE TING
WITHOUT
A-LING

CIRCUS
WITHOUT
RING

CHOIR
WITHOUT
SING

KITTEN
WITHOUT
STRING

FAMILY
WITHOUT
CUDDLING

me
WE WITHOUT YOU?
AN UNTHINKABLE
FATE!

LIKE FOOD
WITHOUT
PLATE

FISHING
WITHOUT
BAIT

WILLS
WITHOUT
KATE

me
~~WE~~ WITHOUT YOU?
A CRAZY
NOTION!

LIKE ISLAND
WITHOUT
OCEAN

SWING
WITHOUT
MOTION

RASH
WITHOUT
LOTION

WITCH
WITHOUT
POTION

LIKE THIEF
WITHOUT
STEAL

BIKE
WITHOUT
WHEEL

POKER
WITHOUT
DEAL

me
WE WITHOUT YOU?
OH ME,
OH MY!

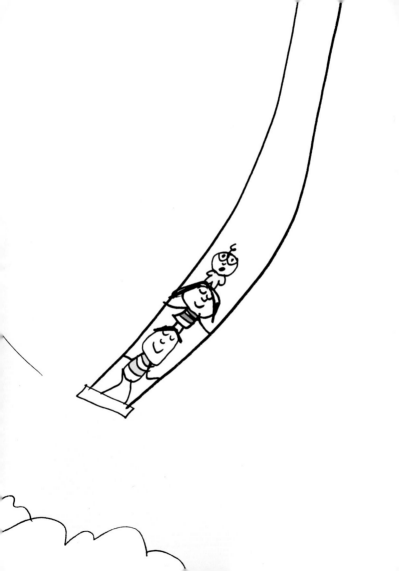

LIKE BATH
WITHOUT
DRY

SHOELACE
WITHOUT
TIE

NEEDLE
WITHOUT
EYE

me
WE WITHOUT YOU?
LIKE RAINBOW
WITHOUT
HUE

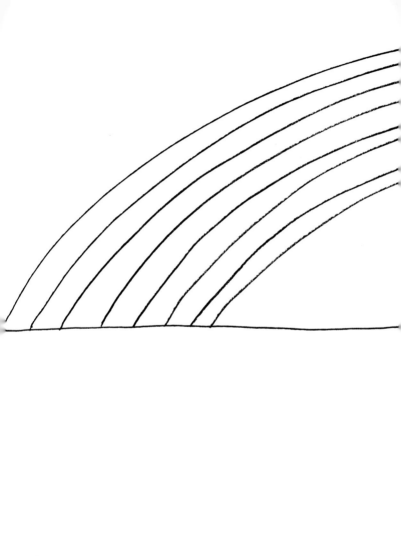

A VERY
SAD
VIEW

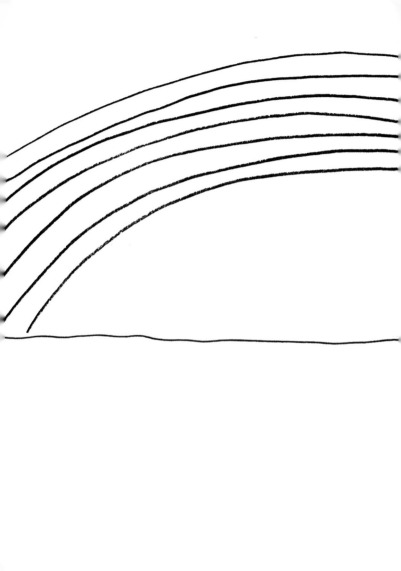

WORK
TO
DO!

GUESS
WHO?

PEEK
A
BOO!

WE ME
WITH
YOU...

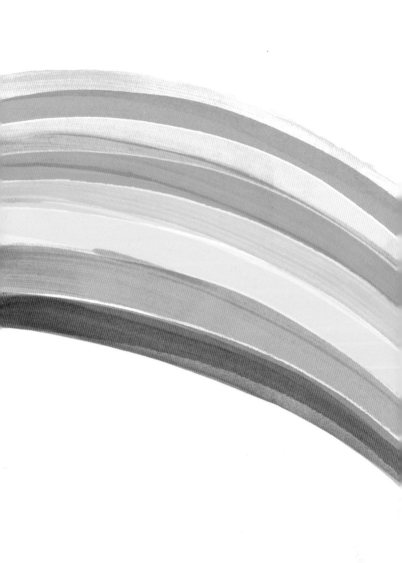

YAHOO!!